# 40 an Understanding of Demons

## T.E. Ferguson Jr., Ph.D.

PublishAmerica
Baltimore

© 2005 by T.E. Ferguson Jr., Ph.D.
All rights reserved. No part of this book may be reproduced, stored in a retrieval system or transmitted in any form or by any means without the prior written permission of the publishers, except by a reviewer who may quote brief passages in a review to be printed in a newspaper, magazine or journal.

First printing

At the specific preference of the author, PublishAmerica allowed this work to remain exactly as the author intended, verbatim, without editorial input.

ISBN: 1-4137-9900-0
PUBLISHED BY PUBLISHAMERICA, LLLP
www.publishamerica.com
Baltimore

Printed in the United States of America

# Introduction

This book was written to help you gain an understanding of what demons are, what they do, what their goals are, and how to get rid of them if you don't want them. Angels are also mentioned in each days reading so you can compare both the good and bad sides of the daily discussion topic. The format used here is that you read a chapter a day and then take some time to think about its content before you read another chapter.

A prayer is listed at the end of each chapter. You can use this prayer or one of your own. The prayer is another tool for you to use to help you understand the topic. The authority on demons is our loving God and there is no one better to ask for help to understand the topic as you journey through this book. You could of course cheat and read more that one days reading material but you won't get the full impact for an understanding of demons.

To best understand demons and the goals that demons wish to achieve we will use as our reference book the Holy Bible. What version of the Bible you use is totally up to you. Some versions are easier to read than others for some people so the choice is up to you. Some people like to read the reference verses in two different versions of the Bible so they can compare them. Many instances regarding demons are recorded in this book and reading the verses in the Bible pertaining to these demons can be very illuminating. The wording of the verses is not included in this book because we want you to use your Bible along with this book. Let the Holy Spirit talk to you as you read God's word.

Several of the scripture verses are repeated during the course of this study. This is done for two reasons. First, the verses contain information that is applicable to several topics. Second, the verses are important for a close walk with Jesus Christ and for our overall spiritual well being. The verses that are repeated are usually verses worth putting to memory.

May God bless you as you study His word and take this journey to learn more about your adversaries, Satan and his demons.

# Dedication

This book is dedicated to Barbara, Holly, and Krystal-Lynn. These three women were a source of encouragement while they waited patiently for me on several occasions to finish reading some piece of data I was analyzing. Countless pages of data were analyzed during the generation of this book and they never once hurried the analytical process.

This book is also dedicated to Pastor Kenneth M. Tapper and his editing skills which helped to make this book possible. A retired preacher never retires to the farm; he just goes out to pastor.

Last but not least, this book is dedicated to the members of my young adults Sunday School class. Many times during the course of a Sunday School lesson I would go off on a tangent about demons or angels and they patiently listened. Sometimes their questions sent me scurrying to do more research, and for that I will always be grateful.

Study your Holy Bible so you can show yourself approved unto God, a workman who can determine the difference between truth and lies. This is how we look at Second Timothy, chapter 2, verse 15.

May the Lord bless you as you read this book and as you open your Bible to read the reference verses that are associated with each days reading.

# 40 Days to an Understanding of Demons

| | | |
|---|---|---|
| Day #1 | What is the origin of Demons? | 11 |
| Day #2 | Do demons exist today and if they do, where can they be found? | 13 |
| Day #3 | Demons have the sense of sight. | 16 |
| Day #4 | Demons have the sense of hearing. | 18 |
| Day #5 | Demons have the ability to speak. | 20 |
| Day #6 | Demons have the ability to obtain and retain knowledge. | 22 |
| Day #7 | Demons can understand and comprehend. | 24 |
| Day #8 | Demons understand fear and can show a reaction to fear. | 26 |
| Day #9 | Demons can cooperate with one another. | 28 |
| Day #10 | Demonic influence can cause a person to have unusual strength. | 30 |
| Day #11 | Demonic influence can cause blindness in a person. | 33 |
| Day #12 | Demonic influence can cause loss of hearing in a person. | 35 |

| | | |
|---|---|---|
| Day #13 | Demonic influence can cause a person to convulse uncontrollably. | 37 |
| Day #14 | Demonic influence can cause a person to lose the ability to speak. | 39 |
| Day #15 | Demonic influence can elevate the level of pride in a person to do evil. | 41 |
| Day #16 | Demonic influence can cause physical abnormalities in a person. | 43 |
| Day #17 | Demonic influence can elevate the level of doubt a person may have. | 45 |
| Day #18 | Demonic influence can elevate the level of greed in a person. | 47 |
| Day #19 | Demonic influence can cause a person to do themselves harm. | 49 |
| Day #20 | Demonic influence can give a person the ability to know things they would have no way of knowing. | 51 |
| Day #21 | Demonic influence can cause a person to refuse to forgive another person. | 53 |
| Day #22 | Demonic influence can cause a person to undergo a severe personality change. | 55 |
| Day #23 | Demonic influence can cause a person to have a disregard for modesty. | 57 |
| Day #24 | Demonic influence can cause a person to avoid normal social interaction. | 59 |

| | | |
|---|---|---|
| Day #25 | Demonic influence can cause a person to lie continuously. | 61 |
| Day #26 | Demons have more wisdom than mankind but are limited in their wisdom. | 63 |
| Day #27 | Demons are more powerful than mankind but are limited in their powers. | 65 |
| Day #28 | Demons are part of God's creation and therefore are under His authority. | 67 |
| Day #29 | Demons do not die. | 69 |
| Day #30 | Demons do not marry. | 71 |
| Day #31 | Demons can be used by God for His purposes. | 73 |
| Day #32 | Demons can affect men, women, children, and animals. | 75 |
| Day #33 | Demons have easy access to a person when sin is present in their life. | 78 |
| Day #34 | Demons have the ability to travel. | 80 |
| Day #35 | Demons know that Jesus Christ is the Son of God. | 82 |
| Day #36 | Demons possess different degrees of wickedness. | 84 |
| Day #37 | Demons can masquerade as good spirits. | 86 |
| Day #38 | Demons can trouble a person and not possess (enter) the person. | 88 |

Day #39   Demons can leave a body and then return       90
          again.

Day #40   Demons can't make you do anything you         92
          don't want to do.

Day #41   Do you think that you are being demonically   94
          influenced?

Conclusion                                              96

# Day #1
## What is the origin of demons?

Please open your Holy Bible to the book of Isaiah, chapter 14, verses 12 through 15 as we begin our study for the day.

Before we answer the question as to the origin of demons we first need to define what a demon is. A definition of a demon in a dictionary would indicate that a demon is an evil spirit. Christian theology would define a demon as an unclean spirit, a bad angel or a fallen angel. For our understanding of what a demon is we will focus on the belief that demons were at one time angels created by God to worship Him. These angels were cast down from heaven to earth along with Lucifer, also known as Satan, when they rebelled against God. Demons, like their leader Lucifer, have the earth on which we live as their environment to create their havoc.

The basis for the belief that demons are fallen angels is taken from the book of Isaiah, chapter 14, verses 12 through 15 where we can find an account of Satan and his rebelling against God. This event is also recorded in the book of Ezekiel, chapter 28, verses 12 through 15.

When we look in the book of Luke, chapter 10, verse 18 we find Jesus talking to seventy people telling them that He saw Satan fall from heaven like lightning. When Satan left heaven he took with him approximately one third of all the angels that existed in heaven at that time. The biblical reference for the previous statement can be found in the book of Revelation, chapter 12, verse 4.

When we look in the Bible to the book of Job, chapters 1 and 2, we find that Satan currently has access to heaven. This will change some time in the future because when we look into the book of Revelation, chapter 12, verses 7 through 9 we find an event that will take place in the future. In these verses we find a conflict will break out in heaven between God and the Devil. Fighting for God will be the archangel Michael and his angels. Fighting for the Devil will be himself and his angles. The Devil (Satan) will fight the battle but will not be successful. As a result of loosing the battle Satan and his followers, the bad angels, will be permanently cast out of heaven. In the book of Matthew, chapter 25, verse 41 we find that hell is waiting for Satan and his angels.

When we compare demons, or "fallen angels", to "good angels" we look at the "good angels" as servants of God. Angels were created by God to serve him. God's angels can serve many different functions. They can be messengers of good news from God or they can bring destruction from our Heavenly Father. The Bible refers to the creation of angels in the book of Psalms, chapter 8, verse 5. This verse indicates to us than man was created by God to be a little lower than angels in the hierarchy of the universe. In Psalms, chapter 148, verse 2 we find angles mentioned and in verse 5 we find once again that God created angels. In the book of Hebrews, chapter 1, verse 14 we find that angels were created by God to minister to all those who accept the gift of salvation.

It is important, as we continue with our study, that we realize any powers given by God to the "good angels" were shared by the "bad angels" before they were thrown out of heaven and landed on earth.

### Prayer for the day:
Our Father in heaven above we thank You for Your "good angels". As we continue with our study we ask Your help to understand the "fallen angels". In the name of Jesus Christ we pray. Amen.

# Day #2

## Do demons exist today and if they do, where can they be found?

Please open your Holy Bible to the book of Luke, chapter 4, verses 33 through 35 as we begin our study for the day.

To determine whether or not demons exist today and where they can be found we will look at our resource book, the Holy Bible, for guidance. If we consider demons as "fallen angels" then we must realize that they were created by God and have existed since that day when God created them.

Demons can be found in humans, in animals, and can be related to inanimate objects.

There are many references in the Bible that refer to demon possession. We will look in the book of Luke for our references. Luke was a physician by trade and therefore knew the difference between a physical aliment and demon possession. In the book of Luke, chapter 4, verses 33 through 35 we find the first case of demon possession that Luke recorded. In these verses we find a demon possessed man in the synagogue. The demon recognized Jesus as the "Holy One of God" and asked Jesus if He was there to destroy him. Jesus told the demon to be quiet and come out of the man. The demon threw the man down and then came out of him without hurting him.

The actions of this man would indicate mental illness to some but the physician Luke records this event as a demon possessed man.

Demon possession of animals can be found in the book of Luke, chapter 8, verses 27 through 33. These verses are very important to our study because they contain many characteristics of demons. In verses 32 and 33 we find that after the demons were cast out of the man they entered the swine. Once they possessed the swine the demons forced the swine to destroy themselves. We must take note that the swine were destroyed and no mention is made in these verses that the demons were also destroyed. For our study we will assume that those demons were not destroyed and are still in existence today.

Demon possession related to inanimate objects can be found in the book of Luke, chapter 8, verse 27. In this verse we find that the demon possessed individual preferred not to wear any cloths, be near tombs of the dead, and actually live among the tombstones. From the location of where the demon possessed man was residing we can assume that the demons like being near the dead and their final resting place.

Once we acknowledge that demons still exist today we also acknowledge that good angels also exist. The battle between good and evil has existed since that day when God ousted Satan and his angels out of heaven.

When Satan appeared in the Garden of Eden and convinced Eve to eat the fruit that changed the course of history he was already evil. See Genesis, chapter 3, verses 1 through 6 for the details of Eve eating the fruit. The fact that Satan was evil in the garden indicates to us he was thrown out of heaven before God created Eve.

One of Satan's tools is that he will lie to you and tell you what you want to hear with the intent of turning you away from God. He will try and convince you that you can make it on your own without any help from God. When you stop and think about it there isn't anyone better to help you live your life than the Creator of both heaven and earth. The reference in the Bible for the creation statement can be found in Genesis, chapter 1, verse 1.

Prayer for the day:
Our Father in heaven above we thank You that You created us and Your angels. We understand that demons and angels can be found anywhere and at any time. We ask that You help us gain an understanding of both the bad and the good angels. In the name of Jesus Christ we pray. Amen.

# Day #3

## Demons have the sense of sight.

Please open your Holy Bible to the book of Matthew, chapter 8, verses 28 and 29 as we begin our study for the day.

Many instances of demons exercising the sense of sight are recorded in the Bible. One of the first instances recorded in the New Testament of the Bible was recorded in the book of Matthew, chapter 8, verses 28 and 29. In these verses we see that the demons used the sense of sight to determine the "Son of God", Jesus Christ, was coming near. A demon using the sense of sight is also recorded in the book of Luke, chapter 4, verses 33 through 35. In these verses we find that a demon possessed man was in the synagogue when Jesus entered. The demons inside the man immediately yelled out to Jesus when they saw him stating that He was the "Holy One of God". They also knew Jesus could destroy them. Jesus told them to be quiet and come out of the man, which they did. A point to realize here is the demons were powerless against Jesus.

The use of the sense of sight by Angels is also quite prevalent in the New Testament of the Bible. In the book of Matthew, chapter 1, verse 20 we find an angel of the Lord appearing to Joseph, the earthly father of Jesus, in a dream. The angel used the sense of sight to call Joseph by name and then tell him not to be afraid to take Mary as his wife. The baby that Mary was to deliver was conceived of the Holy Spirit. Continuing with verse 21 we find that this baby will save His people from their sins.

In the book of Luke, chapter 1, verses 11 through 20 we find the angel Gabriel using the sense of sight to recognize the person he is speaking to as Zacharias. It is interesting to note that in verse 19 this particular angel has a given name. It also raises a question as to whether or not all angels, and demons, have given names. We know that one group of demons carried the name of "Legion" as evidenced in Luke, chapter 8, verse 30. We also know that one angel's name is Gabriel as found in the book of Luke, chapter 1, verse 19 and another angel's name is Michael as found in the book of Jude, chapter 1, verse 9.

We find the angel Gabriel using the sense of sight once again in the book of Luke, chapter 1, verses 30 through 33. In these verses Gabriel used the sense of sight to recognize Mary as he told her that she was going to give birth to Jesus, the Saviour of this world.

In the previously stated book of Jude, chapter 1, verse 9 we find the archangel Michael using the sense of sight to recognize Satan as the person he was speaking to. In this verse the archangel Michael and the leader of all the demons, Satan, are disputing over the body of Moses. In verse 9 we also find Michael did not bring an accusation against Satan, but told Satan that Jesus would rebuke him. When a powerful archangel such as Michael does not bring an accusation against Satan it should tell us something. We should not bring an accusation against Satan, but should tell him the Lord, Jesus Christ, will rebuke him.

Prayer for the day:
Our Father in heaven above we thank You for all those who have received the gift of sight. We ask that all who have received this gift see the things You want them to. Please help everyone with the gift of sight to glorify You with all they see and do. In the name of Jesus Christ we pray. Amen.

# Day #4

## Demons have the sense of hearing.

Please open your Holy Bible to the book of Matthew, chapter 8, verses 31 and 32 as we begin our study for the day.

There are probably just as many instances of demons using the sense of hearing recorded in the Bible as there are for the sense of seeing. The demons that recognized Jesus when they saw him also acknowledged His words when He told them to get out of the person.

An example of Jesus Christ talking to demons can be found in the Bible in the book of Matthew, chapter 8, verses 31 and 32. In verse 31 we find a group of demons begging Jesus to let them go into the herd of swine after they depart from the men. In verse 32 we find where Jesus answered the demons, they heard His words, and they did what they were told to do.

In the book of Luke, chapter 4, verses 33 through 35 we find a demon that recognized Jesus Christ as the Son of God and asked Jesus if He was there to destroy him. In verse 35 we find Jesus speaking to the demon, the demon hears what Jesus tells him, and then leaves the man.

Demons take instructions to torment people from their leader Satan and therefore they hear his instructions. Remember that according to the Bible in the book of John, chapter 12, verse 31 that

Satan is the ruler of this world. Satan has great power on earth but remember also that God is greater than Satan which is stated in the book of First John, chapter 4, verse 4.

Angels take their instructions from God in heaven and therefore hear His instructions. In the book of Luke, chapter 1, verse 19 we find the angel Gabriel speaking to Zacharias. Gabriel states that he normally stands in the presence of God and that he was sent to speak to Zacharias to tell him about the upcoming birth of his son. The instructions that Gabriel received to tell Zacharias came directly from God. Gabriel received the instructions from standing in the presence of God our Father.

Also in the book of Luke, chapter 1, verse 26 we find God sent the angel Gabriel to Nazareth to speak to Mary, the mother of Jesus. Continuing with verse 30 we see that Gabriel told Mary that God has found favor with her. Gabriel heard directly from God that He found favor with Mary. God sent Gabriel from heaven to earth to relay this information to Mary. When we look at the word angel we can relate the word messenger to it because one of the functions of angels is they are God's messengers.

Prayer for the day:
Our Father in heaven above those of us You gave the sense of hearing thank You for that ability. We ask that You help us hear only those things that are pleasing to You. In the name of Jesus Christ we pray. Amen.

# Day #5
## Demons have the ability to speak.

Please open your Holy Bible to the book of Matthew, chapter 8, verse 31 as we begin our study for the day.

Demons have the ability to speak, have spoken, and in several cases their words have been recorded. Looking at one verse again from Day #4 in the book of Matthew, chapter 8, verse 31 we find an example of demons speaking. The demons mentioned in this verse were not only speaking but begging Jesus Christ that if He drove them out of the man's body they be allowed to enter a herd of pigs. The fact that the demons were begging indicates to us that Jesus Christ had full authority over them and they feared Him.

In the book of Mark, chapter 1, verse 34 we find that the demons wanted to speak but Jesus would not let them. This verse indicates to us that Jesus Christ has full power over demons to the point that He can tell them to be quiet. The fact the demons wanted to speak, but Jesus would not let them, is also recorded in the book of Luke, chapter 4, verse 41.

We find a demon using a man to cry out in a loud voice in the book of Luke, chapter 4, verse 33 and 34. In these verses we see that demons can be quite loud and also the fact that demons know Jesus Christ is the Son of God. Verse 34 acknowledges the fact that Jesus could destroy the demons if it was God's will to do so.

When we acknowledge demons have the ability to speak we are also acknowledging good angels have the same ability. In the Bible there are many verses where the words of angels have been recorded. Some of the more popular verses can be found in the book of Matthew. In chapter 1, verse 20 we find that the angel of the Lord told Joseph, in a dream, not to be afraid to marry Mary because the baby was conceived of the Holy Spirit. In chapter 2, verse 13 the angel of the Lord told Joseph, in a dream, to take his family and go to Egypt because Herod wanted to kill Mary's son Jesus. In chapter 2, verse 20 we find the angel of the Lord telling Joseph, in a dream, to go back to the land of Israel because the one who sought to kill Jesus was dead.

Before Jesus Christ was born an angel spoke to Mary. This event is recorded in the book of Luke, chapter 1, verses 30 and 31. An angel also spoke to Joseph before Jesus was born, as was previously mentioned. After the birth of Jesus an angel spoke to the shepherds as recorded in the book of Luke, chapter 2, verses 8 through 11. An angel came to strengthen Jesus after He was tempted by Satan in the wilderness in the book of Matthew, chapter 4, verse 11. It is not recorded in this verse that the angel spoke, but we know that the angel ministered unto Jesus. In the book of Luke, chapter 22, verse 43 we find where an angel strengthened Jesus Christ after one of the times He finished praying at the Mount of Olives. After Jesus arose from the dead an angel spoke to the women at the tomb as recorded in the book of Matthew, chapter 28, verses 5 through 7.

Prayer for the day:

Our Father in heaven above we acknowledge the fact that both demons and angels have the ability to speak. We also acknowledge demons speak lies and angels speak the words You tell them. We ask that You help us to always hear Your words and not those of Satan or his demons. In the name of Jesus Christ we pray. Amen.

# Day #6

## Demons have the ability to obtain and retain knowledge.

Please open your Holy Bible to the book of Acts, chapter 19, verse 15 as we begin our study for the day.

In the book of Acts, chapter 19, verse 15 we find a demon stating that he knows who Jesus is, and he has heard of Paul, but doesn't know who the people are that are trying to perform an exorcism. In the next verse, verse 16, we find that the demon gives the demonically influenced person great strength to give a severe beating to the seven exorcists and to strip them of their clothes.

The demon in this example knew who Jesus was and had heard of the Apostle Paul. There isn't any doubt that the demon knew that Jesus and Paul could chase him out of the man if they were there. This demon demonstrates to us that he had the ability to obtain knowledge about Jesus and Paul and also had the ability to retain the knowledge. The seven men who were trying to do the exorcism didn't have the faith required to do the exorcism and therefore the demon was able to overpower them. Without the shield of faith the evil of this world have the power to overcome. In the book of Ephesians, chapter 6, verse 16 we find it stated that faith is the shield in the battle against Satan and his followers.

In the book of Mark, chapter 5, verse 7 and in the book of Luke, chapter 4, verse 41 we find that demons know that Jesus Christ is the Son of God. These demons knew this fact even though the people who were with Jesus at the time didn't. The people had to come to the realization that Jesus was the Son of God where as the demons already obtained that information and also retained it.

Angels, like demons, have been in existence from the day they were created to the very minute you are reading this and will continue to exist for all eternity. Their data base of knowledge consists of God's direct revelation to them and all the years they have been in existence. Both angels and demons know how mankind will react in different situations and use that information to their advantage. In the Bible in the book of Ecclesiastes, chapter 1, verse 9 we find it stated that there is nothing new under the sun. Over all the years that mankind has been in existence there have been many variations of the sins that were committed earlier in time against God, but nothing new.

Prayer for the day:
Our Father in heaven above we acknowledge the fact that even though demons and angels have acquired a vast amount of knowledge over many years that Your knowledge is not limited to the past but also includes the future. We ask Your help that the knowledge we acquire during our lifetime will be used to honor and glorify Your name. In the name of Jesus Christ we pray. Amen.

# Day #7

## Demons can understand and comprehend.

Please open your Holy Bible to the book of James, chapter 2, verse 19 as we begin our study for the day.

Demons know who God is and understand fully that once they sinned against God they will be punished. They were given the choice to either follow God or Satan and they chose Satan. In the book of James, chapter 2, verse 19 we find that the demons know who God is. In the book of Matthew, chapter 8, verse 29 we see that the demons know Jesus Christ is the Son of God.

Demons fully understand and comprehend that hell is waiting for them because of their actions. In the book of Matthew, chapter 25, verse 41 we see that hell is waiting for Satan and his demonic followers. In the book of Revelation, chapter 12, verse 12 we find that Satan knows his time is short on this earth.

Demons understand that God has full power over them. In the book of Job, chapter 1, verse 12, and in chapter 2, verse 6 we see that the leader of the demons, Satan, was given permission by God to do his evil deeds. In the book of Luke, chapter 8, verse 28 we see that demons comprehend Jesus Christ has the power to torment them if He so desired.

Both the good angels and the demons have studied mankind since creation and understand how they will react in various situations. Demons know what buttons to press to make mankind act in a sinful way. Angels are used by God to help those who have accepted the gift of salvation. In the book of Hebrews, chapter 1, verse 14 we find the biblical reference for the previous statement.

Angels know that Satan's time is limited on this earth as referenced in the book of Revelation, chapter 12, verse 12. Angels know that Jesus will return again to this earth, but they don't know when, as found in the book of Matthew, chapter 24, verse 36, and in the book of Mark, chapter 13, verse 32. They also understand and comprehend that there will be one last great battle some day in the future between good and evil as evidenced in the book of Revelation, chapter 12, verses 7 through 9.

Prayer for the day:

Our Father in heaven above we acknowledge that both the good angels and the demons understand mankind. We thank You that You have total control over both the good angels and the demons and also that You have mankind's best interests at heart. We ask that You continue to help us as we make our journey through life. In the name of Jesus Christ we pray. Amen.

# Day #8
## Demons understand fear and can show a reaction to fear.

Please open your Holy Bible to the book of Matthew, chapter 8, verse 29 as we begin our study for the day.

Examples that demons show fear in the presence of the Son of God can be found in the books of Matthew, Mark, and Luke in the Bible. In the book of Matthew, chapter 8, verse 29 we find that the demons who possessed the man cried out to Jesus to ask him if He was there to torment them before their time. In the book of Mark, chapter 5, verse 7 we find a reiteration of verse 29 in Matthew utilizing the word torment again. The demons recognized Jesus as the Son of God and acknowledged by their fear that He could torment them.

In the book of Luke, chapter 4, verse 34 the demon (unclean spirit) who possessed the man in the synagogue asked Jesus of Nazareth if He was there to destroy him. In the same verse the demon acknowledged the fact that he knew who Jesus was, "the Holy One of God", and was fearful that Jesus would destroy him. In verse 35 the demon quietly came out of the man and left him unharmed.

In the book of James, chapter 2, verse 19 we find that demons believe there is one God and shudder. In order for one to shudder, or tremble, one could assume there is fear connected to the reaction.

It is written in the book of Luke, chapter 12, verses 4 and 5 that we are to fear God. In these two verses the reason why we are to fear God is because men can kill the body but only God has the power to accept a person into heaven or send the person to hell.

In the book of Job, chapter 28, verse 28, we are told if we fear God we show wisdom and if we turn away from evil we show understanding.

In the book of Psalms, chapter 89, verse 7 we find all those who surround God, angels included, fear God.

The fear of God we speak of is not a fear like we might have of, say, a rattlesnake. The fear of God we speak of is a reverential fear with knowledge of how holy and righteous God is. It is acknowledging our unworthiness while acknowledging His total awesomeness.

Prayer for the day:

Our Father in heaven above we thank You that Your powers are so great even the demons respect and fear You. We ask that when we are experiencing fear that You help us overcome it. In the name of Jesus Christ we pray. Amen.

# Day #9

## Demons can cooperate with one another.

Please open your Holy Bible to the book of Genesis, chapter 1, verses 26 and 27 as we begin our study for the day.

One demon will cooperate with another demon, or demons, inside of a human body. They share the common goal of inhabiting and gaining control of the body.

Their supreme commander, Satan, takes great satisfaction when one of God's creations in under demonic control. The ultimate goal of this control is to destroy one of God's creations. Man was made in the image of God; see Genesis, chapter 1, verses 26 and 27. To destroy one of God's creations is analogous to Satan of destroying a piece of God.

One of the more common examples of multiple demons inside a body is the demonic possession of Mary Magdalene. Historically this fact has been recorded in the Bible in book of Mark, chapter 16, verse 9 and in the book of Luke, Chapter 8, verse 2. These verses state that she had seven devils (demons) possessing her.

It is also recorded that Jesus Christ chased the demons from Mary Magdalene. Notice we used the word chased, and not destroyed. It is a critical concept to understand that the demons were removed and not destroyed. The demons that possessed Mary Magdalene are still in existence today. They roam the earth, going from person to person, inhabiting those they can. Their goal today is the same as it was during Mary Magdalene's time. They want to keep as many people as they can from a personal relationship with Jesus Christ.

After the demons were chased from Mary Magdalene her life was changed. She became a follower of Jesus Christ and His teachings and even supported His ministry. Her support of Jesus' ministry is recorded in the book of Mark, chapter 15, verses 40 and 41 and in the book of Luke, chapter 8, verses 1 through 3. We must note that the removal of the demons didn't instantly make her a follower and supporter of Jesus. She still had to accept or reject Jesus Christ. History has recorded that Mary Magdalene choose to accept and follow Jesus.

Angels also cooperate with one another. When we look at the birth of Christ in the Bible in the book of Luke, chapter 2, verses 13 through 15 we find angels praising the birth in unison. We also see in verse 15 when the angels were done praising God they returned back to heaven.

When we look in the book of Genesis, chapter 19, verse 1 we find two of God's good angels were teamed together to visit Lot at the entrance to the city of Sodom.

The difference between demons and angles regarding cooperation is quite evident. Demons work together to destroy God's creatures. Angles work together to praise God, their Creator, and to do His will. Angels help mankind when directed by God to do so and demons try to destroy mankind as directed by their leader Satan.

Prayer for the day:

Our Father in heaven above we know that demons cooperate with one another and we ask that You help us cooperate with other Christian believers so together we can stand united and fight the evil that demons portray. We also thank You that You created angles that You use to help us when we need help. In the name of Jesus Christ we pray. Amen

# Day #10

At the end of this day you will be one quarter of the way to an understanding of demons. So, how are you doing with your study?

## Demonic influence can cause a person to have unusual strength.

Please open your Holy Bible to the book of Luke, chapter 8, verses 27 through 33 as we begin our study for the day.

One instance of demon possession recorded in the Bible indicates that when several demons possess a person they can give that person incredible strength. Details of this instance can be found in the book of Luke, chapter 8, verses 27 through 33. These verses also show us that demons can see, hear, speak, plead, and show signs of fear in the presence of a person that can destroy them. The person that can destroy them is Jesus Christ.

Another instance of demon possession indicates that a demon can throw a person to the ground. This instance can be found in the book of Luke, chapter 9, verse 42. In this verse we find the demon that was living inside the child threw the child to the ground and made him convulse. When we read the book of Luke we must remember that the writer, Doctor Luke, knew the difference between health problems and demon possession. When Doctor Luke tells us that the child was demon possessed we really should believe that he knew what he was talking about.

In the book of Mark, chapter 1, verse 26 we find an incident where Jesus chased a demon out of a person in the synagogue. Before the unclean spirit left the person the spirit cried out with a loud voice and caused the person to convulse.

Lack of knowledge about demonic influences can limit us when we encounter a person who might potentially be demonically influenced. In the book of Second Timothy, chapter 2, verse 15 we are told to study the word of God so, with God's help, we can discern between good and evil.

There are many stories that have been recorded throughout history of people who showed extraordinary strength at a time of crises. Did this strength come from excessive amounts of adrenaline or did it come from angelic help? Did the extra strength come from an angel that was sent by God to help? What you choose to believe is contingent on your faith. A good definition of faith can be found in the book of Hebrews, chapter 11, verse 1 which indicates that faith is the substance behind the things that we hope for, and it is the evidence of things we do not see.

In the Bible we can find an example of a person who showed extraordinary strength after he requested it. The case in point can be found in the book of Judges, chapter 16, verses 28 through 30. In these verses we find Samson asking God to remember him and to give him extraordinary strength. Samson wanted this strength to avenge himself of the Philistines because they removed his eyesight. God granted his request for the extraordinary strength and it is recorded in verse 30 that when the house fell down Samson killed more Philistines that day then he did during his lifetime.

Angels, and demons, have more strength than humans. A good example of an angel showing a great amount of strength can be found in the Holy Bible in the book of Matthew, chapter 28, verse 2. In this verse we find that an angel came down from heaven, rolled the stone away from the entrance of the tomb where the body of Jesus was placed after the crucifixion, and sat on it. This stone at the entrance to the tomb probably weighed several tons.

Prayer for the day:
Our Father in heaven above we know from our study that demons have the characteristic of strength but we also know that Your strength is more powerful than theirs. We also know that You will give us the strength to defeat demons if we believe in You and ask You for Your help. In the name of Jesus Christ we pray. Amen.

# Day #11

## Demonic influence can cause blindness in a person.

Please open your Holy Bible to the book of Matthew, chapter 12, verse 22 as we begin our study for the day.

There are two types of blindness that need to be discussed. The first type is physical blindness. In the Bible we find a man who was blinded by demon possession in Matthew, chapter 12, verse 22. This verse clearly indicates that a man who was blind, mute, and demon possessed was brought to Jesus Christ. Immediately after Jesus healed the man he began to speak and see.

The second type of blindness is spiritual blindness. This type of blindness is mentioned in the Bible in the book of Second Corinthians, chapter 4, verse 4. In this verse we find that Satan, who is the god of this world, blinds the minds of those who follow him so they can not see the good and the glory in Jesus Christ. In Ephesians, chapter 4, verse 18 we find that because of the blindness of their hearts the unbelievers are alienated from having a life with the Heavenly Father. The blindness in this verse is directly related to the ignorance that is in the unbeliever. Satan and his followers do not want you to see the light in Jesus Christ and will do everything in their power to prevent you from doing so. It is recorded in the book of John, chapter 8, verse 12 that Jesus is the light of this world and those that follow Him will not walk in darkness but will walk in the light of life.

When we look in the book of John, chapter 14, verse 6 we see that Jesus Christ said that He is the way, the truth, and the life and that no person can go the God the Father but through Him. Read John, chapter 14, verse 6 substituting the word light for the word life and you will see that Jesus is the truth, the way, and the light. We can make this word substitution based on verses found in the books of John and Psalms. In the book of John, chapter 1, verse 4 we find Jesus is life, and His life is the light of men. In the book of Psalms, chapter 119, verse 105 we find the word of God is a lamp for our feet and a light for our path.

In the Bible in the book of Genesis, chapter 19, verse 11 we find that angels caused men, both large and small, to become blind so they could not find a door. This incident is tied into the destruction of Sodom and Gomorrah which was destroyed by God because of their excessive sinful ways. The full story of the destruction of Sodom and Gomorrah can be found in Genesis, chapter 19, verses 1 through 29.

In Genesis, chapter 19, verse 24 we find that fire and brimstone rained down from heaven to destroy Sodom and Gomorrah. Researchers and geologists have found rocks at the site where Sodom and Gomorrah was that indicates there was a very hot fire there at one point in time.

Prayer for the day:
Our Father in heaven above we acknowledge there are two different types of blindness, physical and spiritual. We understand that physical blindness can prevent us from seeing others and spiritual blindness can prevent us from seeing You. We ask that You help us see what You want us to see and do what You want us to do. In the name of Jesus Christ we pray. Amen.

# Day #12
## Demonic influence can cause loss of hearing in a person.

Please open your Holy Bible to the book of Mark, chapter 9, verses 17 through 27 as we begin our study for the day.

In the book of Mark, chapter 9, verses 17 through 27 we find that a demon was responsible for the loss of hearing in a man's son. In verse 25 we find that Jesus Christ told the deaf and dumb demon to come out of the man's son and not to enter him again. After the demon departed from the man's son the lad appeared to be dead. Jesus reached down with His hand, grasped the young man's hand, and lifted him up.

Demons want to keep you from hearing the word of God. They don't want you to hear the good news that Jesus Christ died on the cross for your sins. When demons hear the name of God's Son it reminds them they are destined to spend eternity in hell for their disobedience against God. In the book of Romans, chapter 10, verse 17 we are told that faith comes from hearing the message of salvation and the message of salvation is heard through the word of God.

We have not found any instances in the Bible where angels are responsible for causing a hearing loss in a person. We have found where angels were responsible for removing sight from people such as in the book of Genesis, chapter 19, verse 11. In this verse we find two angels removing the ability of the young and old to see. We also found where an angel was responsible for removing the ability of a person to speak such as in the book of Luke, chapter 1, verse 20. In this verse the angel Gabriel removed the ability of Zacharias to speak.

Angels hear the words of God and obey Him. In the Bible in the book of Luke, chapter 1, verse 19 we find where the angel Gabriel stands in the presence of God. Gabriel in this case is talking to Zacharias and relaying to him the words that God spoke to him. Angels can stand in the presence of God and hear His words because God created them that way.

Jesus told a large group of people that if they have ears they should listen to what He was preaching. This is recorded in the book of Mark, chapter 4, verse 9. Also in the book of Mark, chapter 4, verse 24 it was recorded that we should be careful of what we hear. We should listen to good things that are spoken and turn away from evil things.

Prayer for the day:

Our Father in heaven above we know that You hear everything we say and see everything do. We ask Your help that when we open up our ears to hear something it will be pleasing to You and whatever we do will also be pleasing to You. In the name of Jesus Christ we pray. Amen.

# Day #13

## Demonic influence can cause a person to convulse uncontrollably.

Please open your Holy Bible to the book of Luke, chapter 9, verse 42 as we begin our study for the day.

In the book of Luke, chapter 9, verse 42 we find that a demon was responsible for making a person convulse uncontrollably. In this verse we find that the demon threw the boy to the ground and caused him to convulse. In the same verse we find that Jesus drove out the demon and healed the child.

When we read verse 42 we must keep in mind that Luke was a medical doctor and knew the difference between a physical problem that would have caused convulsions and demon possession. Doctor Luke made a medical decision that this boy was demon possessed and did not have a physical aliment and recorded it in the Bible as such.

In the book of Mark, chapter 1, verses 23 through 26 we find where Jesus cured a demon possessed man. After Jesus told the demon to depart from the man the demon convulsed the man, cried out with a loud voice, and then departed as Jesus directed.

There are probably many more incidents of people convulsing that were cured by Jesus and not recorded in the Bible. We are led to believe this because of verses like John, chapter 21, verse 25. In this verse we see if everything Jesus did while He was on earth was recorded there would not be enough room on the earth to hold all of the books that could have been written.

We were not able to find any incidents in the Bible where angels caused convulsions in a person, but we did find where an angel made the earth shake. In the Bible in the book of Matthew, chapter 28, verse 2 we find where an angel caused an earthquake. This earthquake caused the stone at the entrance of the tomb where Jesus Christ was buried to roll away.

In the book of Matthew, chapter 27, verse 51 we find where an earthquake made the veil in the temple to tear in two when Jesus Christ yielded His spirit. We are not saying that an angel caused this earthquake, but we are saying that it certainly is possible.

In the book of Acts, chapter 4, verse 31 it was recorded that after a group of people finished praying, the place where they were meeting was shaken. After the meeting place was shaken they were filled with the Holy Spirit and boldly spoke the word of God. Once again we are not saying that an angel made the room shake, but we are saying that it is certainly a possibility.

Prayer for the day:

Our Father in heaven above we acknowledge that demons can cause convulsions and that the good angels can make the earth shake. We thank You that You are more powerful than both the demons and the good angels and that You help us when we need help. In the name of Jesus Christ we pray. Amen.

# Day #14
## Demonic influence can cause a person to lose the ability to speak.

Please open your Holy Bible to the book of Matthew, chapter 9, verse 32 as we begin our study for the day.

In the book of Matthew, chapter 9, verse 32 we find a man who was demon possessed and could not speak. In verse 33 we find that after Jesus drove the demon out of the man he could then speak. The same story was recorded by Dr. Luke in the book of Luke, chapter 11, verse 14. Doctor Luke's record of the story is important to us because he was a physician and knew the difference between a physical problem and a demon-possessed person. Both Matthew and Dr. Luke recorded the same problem with the same result. Jesus cured the man and he spoke.

In the book of Mark, chapter 9, verse 17 we find a man whose son could not speak. As we continue to read verse 18 we find that this demon also caused the gentleman's son to gnash his teeth, foam at the mouth, be thrown to the ground, and become rigid. Still looking at verse 18 we also see that the disciples could not drive the demon out of boy. Lack of faith on the part of the disciples would not allow them to chase the demon out of the boy. When Jesus took control of the situation He chastised the disciples for their lack of faith as found in verse 19. It is stated in the Bible in the book of Matthew, chapter 21, verse 21 that the power in faith can move mountains. We must carry with us at all times the faith that Jesus is the Son of God and that belief in Him is the only way that we will ever move mountains.

There is even an instance in the Bible where the angel Gabriel was directed by God to remove the ability to speak from Zacharias because of his lack of faith. In the book of Luke, chapter 1, verse 20 we find that Gabriel removed the ability to speak from Zacharias until the birth of his son. In verse 63 we find that Zacharias wrote the name John on the tablet and in verse 64 he started speaking and praising God. The child John referred to here is John the Baptist who foretold the people that their Lord was coming and that He would baptize them with the Holy Spirit.

Prayer for the day:
Our Father in heaven above we thank You that You gave some of us the ability to speak and we ask that the words we speak be pleasing to You. Those of us that You did not give the ability to speak praise You knowing that if we accept Your Son we will be able some day to speak to You in heaven. In the name of Jesus Christ we pray. Amen.

# Day #15

## Demonic influence can elevate the level of pride in a person to do evil.

Please open your Holy Bible to the book of Isaiah, chapter 14, verses 13 and 14 as we begin our study for the day.

In the book of Isaiah, chapter 14, verses 13 and 14 it is recorded that one of the reasons why Satan was kicked out of heaven was because of his pride. In the book of First Timothy, chapter 3, verse 6 we find that to be a bishop in the church the person should not be full of pride less they fall into sin like the devil. If you are currently full of pride you are opening yourself up for a demon that specializes in pride to increase your level to the point that Satan can take over control of your life.

In the book of First Timothy, chapter 6, verse 10 it is clearly stated the love of money is the root of all evil. In many instances the sin of pride accompanies the love of money. If you love money, have a lot of it, and are proud of that fact, you are opening yourself up to possession by the demon of pride. The demon who specializes in pride might invite other demons to join him such as the demon of lying or the demon of stealing. Jesus Christ stated in the book of Matthew, chapter 19, verse 23 that it was harder for a person with a large amount of money to enter heaven than it was for a person with a small amount of money. In the book of Hebrews, chapter 13, verse 5 we are told to keep our lives free from the love of money and to be content with what we have. Having a lot of money is not a sin but loving that money more than God is.

In the Bible in the book of Psalms, chapter 10, verse 4 we find that the proud do not seek God. The verse continues with the fact that God isn't in any of their thoughts.

The good angels are more powerful than mankind and could be proud of that fact, but they are not. The opposite of pride is humility. We see that the good angels would not fill you full of pride because God opposes the proud and gives grace to those who exhibit humility. In the Bible in the book of Proverbs, chapter 3, verse 34 we find that God gives grace to the humble. In the book of James, chapter 4, verse 6 we find the verse in Proverbs is repeated with the fact that God resists the proud and gives grace to the humble. Also in the book of First Peter, chapter 5, verse 5 we find that we should exhibit humility because God resists the proud and gives grace to the humble. The good angles would never lead you to do something that is not pleasing to your Heavenly Father.

Prayer for the day:
Our Father in heaven above we thank You that if we exhibit humility You bless us with Your grace. We ask that You help us have humility and not become proud with any accomplishments that we might have. In the name of Jesus Christ we pray. Amen.

# Day #16
## Demonic influence can cause physical abnormalities in a person.

Please open your Holy Bible to the book of Luke, chapter 13, verse 11 as we begin our study for the day.

In the book of Luke, chapter 13, verse 11 we find a woman who was demon-possessed and the demon would not allow the woman to straighten up. The woman had this condition for eighteen years before she met Jesus Christ. In verses 12 and 13 we find that Jesus healed her and she could then straighten up.

In the book of Job, chapter 2, verse 7 we find that Satan gave Job sore boils from the top of his head to the bottom of his feet. It is important for us to realize that Satan gave Job the boils after he received permission from God to do so. In Job, chapter 2, verse 6 God told Satan that he could harass Job's health but could not take Job's life. In Job, chapter 1, verse 12 we find that God told Satan he could take away all of Job's earthly possessions but could not lay a finger on Job.

It should be very comforting to us that Satan with all the powers he has on earth can't do anything without God's permission. In the book of First Corinthians, chapter 10, verse 13 we find a promise from God that, as believers in Jesus Christ, He will not tempt us beyond what we are able to handle. Whatever problems come your way, you and your Heavenly Father can handle them together. You have God's promise.

If you take the time to search the Bible for an incident where an angel entered and possessed a human body you will not find one. Angels do not possess human bodies to cause physical abnormalities. Angels can, and do, appear in the form of a man but do not use possession to do so.

There are several examples of angels appearing in human form. One of the earliest examples of angels appearing in human form can be found in the book of Genesis, chapter 19, verse 1. In this verse we find two angels appearing in human form. These angels appear to Lot at the gate of the city of Sodom. Continuing with verses 2 and 3 we find Lot persuading the angels to go to his home. The angels go to Lot's home where he provides a feast and unleavened bread for them and they did eat.

Another example of an angel appearing in human form can be found in the book of Mark, chapter 16, verses 5 and 6. In these verses we find an angel appearing as a young man, wearing a long white robe, talking to the ladies at the empty tomb. The tomb is empty at that point in time because Jesus Christ arose from the dead.

Prayer for the day:

Our Father in heaven above we acknowledge that some physical abnormalities can be caused by demonic influences. We also acknowledge that You use some of these physical abnormalities to show Your love, grace, and power. We ask that no matter what physical problems may come our way we never loose our faith in You. In the name of Jesus Christ we pray. Amen.

# Day #17
## Demonic influence can elevate the level of doubt a person may have.

Please open your Holy Bible to the book of Genesis, chapter 3, verses 4 and 5 as we begin our study for the day.

One of the greatest weapons that Satan has in his arsenal is doubt. If he can take your doubts and elevate them to such a high level that you start doubting the very existence of God, he can step in with his lies.

One of the first instances of raising the level of doubt in a person is recorded in the book of Genesis, chapter 3, verses 4 and 5. Here we find that Satan convinces Eve, using the tool of doubt, she won't die if she takes a bite of the fruit. He lies to her and tells her God is afraid that if Eve takes a bite that she will become like Him. In the book of John, chapter 8, verse 44 we find that Satan is a liar and that he is a master in the art of lying.

One of the duties of good angels is they can give confidence to a person. In the Bible in the book of Acts, chapter 27, verses 23 and 24 we find an angel gave the Apostle Paul confidence. In verse 23 Paul tells the group of men an angel of God whom he serves visited him. In verse 24 Paul tells the men that everyone will survive the pending shipwreck.

Angels give comfort to people by telling them to "fear not" and then give them some good news to make them happy. In the book of Genesis, chapter 21, verse 17 we find and angel telling Hagar to "fear not" because God heard the voice of the child. In the book of Matthew, chapter 1, verse 20 we find and angel telling Joseph to "fear not" and marry Mary, the mother of Jesus. Continuing in Matthew, chapter 28, verse 5 we find an angel telling the women to "fear not" because they were looking for the body of Jesus and they could not find it because He had risen from the dead. Doctor Luke writes in the book of Luke, chapter 1, verse 13 that an angel told Zacharias to "fear not" because his prayer was heard and his wife Elizabeth was going to give birth to a son. Continuing in the book of Luke, chapter 1, verse 30 we find an angel telling Mary, the mother of Jesus, to "fear not" because she found favor with God. In the book of Luke, chapter 2, verse 10 we find an angel telling the shepherds tending their flock in the fields to "fear not" because Christ their Saviour was born in Bethlehem.

In the book of Mark, chapter 9, verse 23 we are told all things are possible if we only believe. To fully believe we can not have doubts. To fully believe we must have the faith that whatever we are trying to accomplish will happen, as long as it is God's will.

Prayer for the day:

Our Father in heaven above we thank You for Your good angels and the fact that when we need a dose of confidence You use them. We know that all things are possible if we only believe and we ask that You help us to limit our doubts and to keep our faith and trust in You. In the name of Jesus Christ we pray. Amen.

# Day #18
## Demonic influence can elevate the level of greed in a person.

    Please open your Holy Bible to the book of Luke, chapter 22, verses 1 through 6 as we begin our study for the day.

    If having everything is everything to a person then they are open to demonic influence by a demon that specializes in greed. The demon will use his favorite tactic of lying to tell the person that if they get everything they want they will be happy. If they get everything they certainly won't need God.

    One of the twelve disciples had a problem with greed to the point that Satan entered his body because of his problem. It was after Satan entered his body that the disciple went to the chief priests and captains to help them arrest Jesus for thirty pieces of silver. The name of this disciple was Judas Iscariot and this historical event was recorded in the book of Luke, chapter 22, verses 1 through 6.

    In the book of John, chapter 12, verse 6 we find that Judas was the keeper of the money box for the group of disciples that traveled with Jesus. Judas took out of the money box whatever money was put in it. Judas was greedy for money. The Bible clearly states in the book of First Timothy, chapter 6, verse 10 that the love of money is the root of all evil which was mentioned in our day number 15 reading related to pride.

God knows our needs and in the Bible there are instances recorded where God sent one or more of his angles to take care of the need. One such instance is recorded in the book of Matthew, chapter 4, verse 11. In this verse we find that the angels came and ministered to God's Son, Jesus Christ, after Satan tempted Jesus three times to follow and worship him. The three temptations of Jesus Christ by Satan can be found in the book of Matthew, chapter 4, verses 1 through 11.

When we pray the Lord's Prayer found in the book of Luke, chapter 11, verses 2 through 4 we are asking God to supply us with our daily needs. In verse 3 we specifically ask God to supply us with bread for the day. Notice that it is bread for the day, not bread for the week. Each day we are to pray to our Father for our daily needs.

In the book of First Kings, chapter 19, verses 5 and 6 we find an angel provided bread and water for Elijah. Continuing with verse 7 we find the angel came back a second time and told Elijah to eat.

In our day number 15 reading we learned that we should be content with what we have. Our reference verse for the previous statement can be found in Hebrews, chapter 13, verse 5. If we are content with what God has given us we are one step closer in staying away from greed.

Prayer for the day:
Our Father in heaven above we ask that You help us not to become greedy. We ask that You help us be content with whatever You give us. You know our needs and provide them accordingly. You taught us to pray asking for our daily needs and we thank You for everything You do for us. We pray this prayer in the name of Jesus Christ. Amen.

# Day #19

## Demonic influence can cause a person to do themselves harm.

Please open your Holy Bible to the book of Matthew, chapter 17, verse 15 as we begin our study for the day.

In the book of Matthew, chapter 17, verse 15 we find that a demon possessing a young child caused the child to often fall into fire and water.

In the book of Mark, chapter 5, verse 5 we find a demon-possessed man who lived in the mountains and tombs, crying out, and doing bodily harm to himself by cutting his skin with sharp stones.

The prince of these demons, Satan, wants to destroy your body because you are made in the image of God. In the book of Genesis, chapter 1, verses 26 and 27 we find we are indeed made in the image of God. So, if Satan destroys a body he must feel like he has destroyed a piece of God.

Angels have been sent by God to prevent physical bodies from harm. In the Bible in the Old Testament book of Daniel, chapter 3, verse 25 we find that three men were protected from being consumed by flames by an angel of the Lord. Continuing in chapter 3 with verse 28 we find that God sent his angel to protect the three men from harm because they believed in Him and placed their faith in Him.

Also, in the Old Testament book of Daniel, chapter 6, verses 16 through 23 we find the servant of God, Daniel, being protected in a den of lions by an angel of God. Verse 22 informs us that the angel kept the mouths of the lions closed so they could not cause any bodily harm to Daniel.

When we think of angels protecting us we have a tendency to think of guardian angels. In the book of Psalms, chapter 91, verse 11 we find angels in charge of you and helping you in all that you do. In Matthew, chapter 18, verse 10 we find angels in charge of little children and these angels always see the face of God in heaven. Turn back to the book of Psalms, chapter 34, verse 7 and you will see the angel of the Lord is near those who fear the Lord and this angel also helps them. In the book of Hebrews, chapter 1 verse 14 we see the good angels are ministering spirits that help those who accept Jesus Christ as their personal Saviour.

Prayer for the day:

Our Father in heaven above we thank You that Your good angels protect those who have accepted Your gift of salvation. We ask that You keep Your good angels near to those who believe in You and the bad angels far away. In the name of Jesus Christ we pray. Amen.

# Day #20

At the end of today's reading you will be at the halfway point to an understanding of demons.

## Demonic influence can give a person the ability to know things they would have no way of knowing.

Please open your Holy Bible to the book of Acts, chapter 16, verse 16 as we begin our study for the day.

In the book of Acts, chapter 16, verse 16 we find a slave girl who was responsible for generating large sums of money for her masters by forecasting the future. The verse clearly states that a spirit was responsible for the forecasting. Since we know only God alone knows the future we can safely assume that God was behind any accurate forecasted information that she shared. As we continue reading in Acts, chapter 16, verse 18 we find that Paul chased the spirit out of the girl in the name of Jesus Christ. In verse 19 her masters were very angry that the source of their wealth could no longer forecast the future. In verses 20 through 23 we find both Paul and Silas were beaten and placed in prison. If you read the remainder of chapter 16 you will find Paul and Silas singing hymns, an earthquake that opened the prison doors, an attempted suicide, a man interested in salvation, an act of kindness, and a release from prison. Quite an interesting story to read that started with a slave girl who was demonically influenced.

    Angels know of events that will happen before mankind does. The angel that told Mary she was going to conceive and give birth to Jesus knew before Mary did. Because angels stand in the presence of God, and God tells them what to tell His people, they have the information first. In the Bible in the book of Luke, chapter 1, verse 31 we find where the angel told Mary she was going to give birth to a son and to name him Jesus.

    The two angels that visited Lot in the book of Genesis, chapter 19, verse 1 knew the cities of Sodom and Gomorrah were going to be destroyed before Lot did and were sent to get Lot and his family out of there before the destruction.

Prayer for the day:

Our Father in heaven above we thank You that You love us and that You always know what is best for us. We also thank You that You send Your angels with messages of comfort and hope. We ask that You help us to do what is pleasing to You and to keep the demonic forces away from us. In the name of Jesus Christ we pray. Amen.

# Day #21

## Demonic influence can cause a person to refuse to forgive another person.

Please open your Holy Bible to the book of Second Corinthians, chapter 2, verses 10 and 11 as we begin our study for the day.

In the book of Second Corinthians, chapter 2, verses 10 and 11 we find the Apostle Paul discussing forgiveness. In our natural sinful nature we don't like to forgive. Sometimes we find it easier to hold a grudge than to forgive. On occasions we hold a grudge for so long we tend to forget why we are holding the grudge. In Second Corinthians, chapter 2, verse 11 we see that Satan and his demons look for this flaw in our character. Demonic influences can build on this non-forgiving attitude and turn it into hatred. The hatred can turn into anger and the anger into revenge and even violence. Once the door is opened because of a non-forgiving attitude the demonic forces have no problem capitalizing on it.

You can't be full of hatred and love God. The two can't exist side by side. In the book of Ephesians, chapter 4, verse 32 we are told to forgive one another just as Jesus Christ forgave. When Jesus was on the cross he asked His Father to forgive those who crucified Him because they did not know what they were doing. The reference for the previous statement can be found in the book of Luke, chapter 23, verse 34.

The realization that Jesus Christ forgave your sins becomes very real when you become a Christian. Once you confess your sins to Jesus and he forgives them, removal of the weight of them will make you feel great. Think about it, if Jesus Christ can forgive all your sins with no strings attached the least you can do is forgive others.

Angels do not forgive sins and are not to be worshiped. In the Bible in the book of Revelation, chapter 22, verses 8 and 9 we find where John started to worship an angel and the angel told John not to worship him. The angel told John to consider him a brother and only worship God.

In the book of Matthew, chapter 6, verses 14 and 15 we find where God forgives. In the book of Colossians, chapter 3, verse 13 we are told to forgive one another just as Jesus Christ forgave us.

How many times should we forgive a person? The apostle Peter asked this question in the book of Matthew, chapter 18, verses 21 and 22 and was told to forgive not up to seven times, but seventy times seven times. It is hard for us to imagine forgiving a person four hundred and ninety times. If we were to forgive a person that many times we might at some point during the forgiving process forget what we were forgiving the person for.

### Prayer for the day:

Our Father in heaven above we thank You that You sent Your only begotten Son to die on the cross for our sins. We also thank You that You are a patient God, willing to forgive us when we do wrong. We ask that You help us forgive others as You forgive us. In the name of Jesus Christ we pray. Amen.

# Day #22

## Demonic influence can cause a person to undergo a severe personality change.

Please open your Holy Bible to the book of First Samuel, chapter 16, verses 14 and 15 as we begin our study for the day.

In the book of First Samuel, chapter 16, verses 14 and 15 we find and evil spirit troubling King Saul after the Spirit of the Lord left him. When we look at verse 21 in chapter 16 we find that King Saul loved David. In First Samuel, chapter 18, verses 10 and 11 we find an evil spirit attacking King Saul to the point that he threw a javelin at David in an attempt to kill him. Looking at verse 29 in chapter 18 we find that King Saul became David's enemy all of the time. In First Samuel, chapter 19, verses 9 and 10 we find the evil spirit attacking King Saul and once again he wants to kill David with the javelin. These verses give us evidence that King Saul would go through a personality change every time he was under demonic influence. King Saul's mood changed from normal to abnormal because the evil spirit gave him a strong desire to kill David, who was to be the next King of Israel.

The good angels do not inhabit human bodies to cause personality changes. The good angels can bring a positive answer back from God that could put a person in a good mood and a smile on their face. In the Bible in the book of Acts, chapter 12, verse 5 we find Peter was in prison and the church was in constant prayer for his well being. Continuing with verses 6 through 10 we find an angel from God came and set Peter free and they walked out of the prison together. If you continue reading with verse 12 you will see that Peter went to a house where they were gathered together to pray. In verse 15 a girl named Rhoda is accused of seeing Peter's angel and in verse 16 they opened the door and saw Peter standing there.

It is comforting to know that in the book of Hebrews, chapter 13, verse 8 it tells us Jesus Christ is the same yesterday, today, and forever. If we take this verse and relate it to angels we could say that the good angels did what God told them yesterday, today, and will continue to do so until Jesus Christ comes again.

Prayer for the day:

Our Father in heaven above we acknowledge that demonic influences can cause severe personality changes in a person who is living in sin. We thank You that You send Your good angels with answers to some of our prayers which in turn make us happy. We ask that You help us to stay in constant prayer with You so You can guide us through this life's journey. In the name of Jesus Christ we pray. Amen.

# Day #23

## Demonic influence can cause a person to have a disregard for modesty.

Please open your Holy Bible to the book of Luke, chapter 8, verse 27 as we begin our study for the day.

In the book of Luke, chapter 8, verse 27 we find a man who was possessed by many demons. Doctor Luke recorded that this demon possessed man did not like to wear any clothes. Not only did he not like to wear any clothes but he also liked to live among the tombs.

When we look at society today we find a billion dollar pornography industry. The individuals involved in this industry certainly have no aversion to taking their clothes off and keeping them off. Due to the large number of people taking part in this industry one can't help but think that there are legions of demonic forces actively at work. These demonic forces appear to be active in sex issues as well as the modesty issue.

In the book of Second Samuel, chapter 11, verse 2 we find that one evening while King David was walking around the roof of his palace he saw a very beautiful women bathing. Later in the story King David has her husband sent to the front lines of a battle so he would be killed in action and King David could marry the widow. This is a perfect example of looking, lusting, and conspiracy to commit murder. The story has a happy ending because King David realizes what he did, was genuinely sorry for his sins, asked God for forgiveness, and was granted forgiveness by God. If we are genuinely sorry for our sins, believe that Jesus Christ died for our sins, and are willing to stop our evil ways, God our Heavenly Father will forgive us. We are not saying that the woman was demonically influenced as related to her bathing, but we are saying that watching a women bathing could lead to many sins.

When we look in the Bible at all of the verses that pertain to angels we will not find any references to angels without clothes. The very second the Lord God made clothes for Adam and Eve and clothed them in the book of Genesis, chapter 3, verse 21 we can safely assume that men and women were to wear clothes from that second on. Why did Adam and Eve cover themselves with fig leaves immediately after they sinned in Genesis, chapter 3, verse 7? Scholars believe that they were so ashamed of themselves that they covered themselves.

Also in the book of Genesis, chapter 9, verses 21 through 27 we get the impression from reading these verses that it was shameful for Noah's sons to accidentally see their father without clothes.

Prayer for the day:

Our Father in heaven above, we thank You that even after Adam and Eve sinned You took time to make clothes for them to wear. We ask that You help us to be modest in appearance in Your eyes and to let us be an example to those who have lost the ability to be modest. In the name of Jesus Christ we pray. Amen.

# Day #24

## Demonic influence can cause a person to avoid normal social interaction.

Please open your Holy Bible to the book of Mark, chapter 5, verse 4 as we begin our study for the day.

In the book of Mark, chapter 5, verse 4 we find a demon possessed man who could not be controlled by the use of restraining chains. The verse continues with the fact that the man could not be tamed. It appears this man did not want any social contact and would break the chains to run away and go to the tombs in a graveyard to get away from people. This demon possessed man wanted to be left alone.

Isolation is one of the tools Satan can use to keep you away from God. When you are around people that have the love of Jesus Christ in them and share that love with you, Satan stands a good chance of loosing control of you. If Satan manages to keep you isolated from people that are willing to share the love of Jesus Christ with you then Satan can keep you under his control. Jesus doesn't want to loose you to Satan so Satan will do everything in his power to keep you away from the word of God and from people who share God's word. Reading God's word, the Holy Bible, will allow the Holy Spirit to work in your life to lead you to the love of Jesus Christ.

Angels interact with one another and also with mankind. In the Bible in the book of Luke, chapter 2, verses 13 through 15 we find where a multitude of angels appeared to a group of shepherds watching their flocks. This multitude of angels praised God about the birth of His Son and then went back to heaven.

Christians are to gather together to praise God. In the book of Hebrews, chapter 10, verse 25 we find we are not to avoid assembling together to praise God. We also find in the book of Matthew, chapter 18, verse 20 that whenever two or more are gathered together to praise Jesus Christ, He is there with them.

When Jesus was in the wilderness, alone for forty days, Satan attacked Him three times near the end of His fasting. The three temptations Jesus endured can be found in the book of Matthew, chapter 4, verses 3 through 10. At the conclusion of His temptations the good angels came to attend to Him as found in verse 11.

Prayer for the day:
Our Father in heaven above we thank You for churches where people can gather together to worship and praise You and Your Son. We ask that You help keep within us a strong desire to worship You and spread the good news to all mankind. In the name of Jesus Christ we pray. Amen.

# Day #25

## Demonic influence can cause a person to lie continuously.

Please open your Holy Bible to the book of John, chapter 8, verse 44 as we begin our study for the day.

The Bible is very specific that Satan is the father of all lies. In the book of John, chapter 8, verse 44 you will see Satan does not stand for truth because there is no truth in him. The verse states that Satan is a liar and the father of all lies. Since his demons follow his commands, they will be liars also. When a person starts lying frequently, and sin is getting a good stronghold in their life, the demon who specializes in lying can step in. A person under the demonic influence of lying will lie continuously. They will get to the point where they can not tell the difference between truth and lies because lying has become first nature to them.

An interesting example of Satan filling a person with lies can be found in the book of Acts, chapter 5, verse 3. In this verse we find Peter asks Ananias why Satan has filled his heart to lie to the Holy Spirit. Continue reading to verse 5 and you will find that Ananias was struck down dead as a result of his lying. Just think, what if the next time you tell a lie you are struck down dead? Thank God in heaven above for his mercies.

Christians worship God in spirit and truth as found in the book of John, chapter 4, verses 23 and 24. God stands for truth and Satan and his demons stand for lies.

When we consider angels as God's messengers we know that angels don't lie because God doesn't lie. In the Bible in the book of Psalms, chapter 103, verse 20 we see that the angels listen to the voice of God and do what He tells them to do. When we look in the book of John, chapter 4, verses 23 and 24 we see we must worship God in spirit and in truth. It was also recorded in the book of John, chapter 14, verse 6 Jesus told us He was the way, the truth, and the life and no man can go to God the Father but through Him.

When God gave Moses the Ten Commandments in the book of Exodus, chapter 20 He told us in verse 16 we should not tell lies about our neighbors. The angels in heaven were quite aware of what God wrote on the tablets and knew that the rules applied to them also. Stop and think for a minute what the world would be like if everyone told the truth.

Prayer for the day:

Our Father in heaven above we thank You that You are patient with us and show us mercy when we don't tell the truth. You have told us that if we ask for forgiveness You will forgive. We ask that You help us in our daily walk to tell the truth and not to tell lies. In the name of Jesus Christ we pray. Amen.

# Day #26

## Demons have more wisdom than mankind but are limited in their wisdom.

    Please open your Holy Bible to the book of Second Samuel, chapter 14, verse 20 as we begin our study for the day.

    When we look in the book of Second Samuel, chapter 14, verse 20 we find a wise person whose wisdom was according to an angel of God. We were told by a bible scholar many years ago that knowledge comes from reading books and wisdom comes from God. Both demons and angels were created by God with a specific amount of wisdom that God gave them. Nowhere in the Bible do we find that the angels, bad or good, were created in the image of God. We know from the book of Genesis, chapter 1, verses 26 and 27 that man was created in the image of God.

    Demons use their wisdom to torment people and drive them further away from God their Father. Remember that demons can't do anything without God's permission. If you have sin in your life which is keeping you from a personal relationship with Jesus Christ, then you are opening the door to demonic influences. God loves all people, but hates all sin.

    In the Bible in the book of Ecclesiastes, chapter 1, verse 9 we find that there is nothing new under the sun. The sins that are looked upon as new today are really variations of old sins. Demons have been in existence witnessing all the various types of sins committed and know how to manipulate people to keep them sinning.

The good angels are limited in their wisdom as evidenced in the book of Matthew, chapter 24, verse 36. In this verse we find that the angels in heaven do not know when the second coming of Jesus Christ will be. The angel that spoke to Zacharias in the book of Luke, chapter 1, verse 13 told him not to be afraid because his prayer was heard and his wife was going to give birth to a son. This angel had the wisdom from God that Zacharias' wife was going to give birth to a son. This angel took this wisdom given to him from God and went to Zacharias as God's messenger to bring him the good news. When we look in the book of James, chapter 1, verses 5 and 6 we find that if we are lacking wisdom all we have to do is ask our Heavenly Father for it as long as we have the faith that we will receive it.

As we all know, mankind's knowledge is limited. If you have ever worked on researching a family tree you know what we mean. Most of the time there is limited information. Sometimes you will find a person who wrote some of the information down and possibly a few pictures. Most of the time there is limited information available. Thank God that He gave us the Bible. His word is as valid today as when it was written down. In the book of Hosea, chapter 14, verse 9 we find that the way of the Lord is the right way. The righteous people walk in the ways of the Lord but those who follow Satan stumble in them. Walk in the ways of the Lord.

### Prayer for the day:

Our Father in heaven above we thank You that You told us that if we are lacking wisdom all we have to do is ask You for it. If we believe that we shall receive wisdom from You, we shall receive it. We pray that any wisdom You give us will be used to show You honor and glory. In the name of Jesus Christ we pray. Amen.

# Day #27

## Demons are more powerful than mankind but are limited in their powers.

Please open your Holy Bible to the book of Second Peter, chapter 2, verse 11 as we begin our study for the day.

In the book of Second Peter, chapter 2, verse 11 we find that angels are greater in power and might than mankind. Since we are looking at demons as "fallen angels" then we must look at demons as having more power and might than mankind. However, demons and angels are limited in their powers due to the fact that God created them. In the book of Psalms, chapter 148, verse 5 we find that the angels were created when God commanded that they should be. In the book of Colossians, chapter 1, verse 16 we find everything was created by God for His use.

Demons use their powers to kill mankind indirectly, and not directly. Demonic possession can be strong enough to influence a person to kill another person, or to kill themselves. Always remember the word of God is sharper than any double-edged sword as recorded in Hebrews, chapter 4, verse 12. Once you accept Jesus Christ as your personal Saviour, faith in Him will be your shield against the powers of Satan and his followers. The Bible reference for the previous statement can be found in First Peter, chapter 1, verse 5.

There are many instances recorded in the Bible of powerful angels. One of the more common instances can be found in the book of Matthew, chapter 28, verse 2 where we find an angel rolled back the stone that covered the front of the tomb where Jesus Christ was placed after he was crucified. Another instance can be found in the book of Acts, chapter 5, verse 19 where we find an angel opened the prison doors so the apostles could leave the prison.

In the book of Second Thessalonians, chapter 1, verse 7 we find reference to the Lord Jesus Christ and His mighty (powerful) angels. In the book of Psalms, chapter 103, verse 20 we find reference to the Lord's angels who do what they are told to do and who excel in strength.

When we look into the book of Isaiah, chapter 37, verse 36 we find an angel of the Lord that was powerful enough to kill 185,000 soldiers in one event. The good angels are very powerful and have the ability to end human life if God commands them to do so. Hebrews, chapter 6, verse 13 tells us no one is greater than God. In Ephesians, chapter 1, verse 19 we find that God gives power to those who believe in Him.

Prayer for the day:

Our Father in heaven above we thank You that You created the good angels who are powerful and help mankind when it needs help. We ask for Your help and strength that only You can give to deal with the "fallen angels". In the name of Jesus Christ we pray. Amen.

# Day #28
## Demons are part of God's creation and therefore are under His authority.

Please open your Holy Bible to the book of Psalms, chapter 148, verse 5 as we begin our study for the day.

When we look at demons as "fallen angels" we must look at the fact that God initially created all of the angels as "good angels" and Satan changed that fact. When we look in the book of Psalms, chapter 148, verse 5 we see that all God had to do was command the angels be created and they were. In the book of Colossians, chapter 1, verse 16 we see that God created all things that are in heaven and on earth and everything that is visible and invisible.

The book of Job contains several examples that God has authority over Satan, and in turn over the demons. In the book of Job, chapter 1, verse 12 we see that Satan is given permission by God to torment Job by taking away his worldly possessions. The only stipulation God placed on Satan was that Satan could not put a hand on Job. In Job, chapter 2, verse 6 we find God gave Satan permission to cause severe pain to Job's body. The stipulation given by God this time to Satan was that Satan could not take Job's life. Through it all Job remained faithful to God and Satan lost the arguments he presented to God.

The authority of God over Satan and his angels is clearly indicated in the book of Matthew, chapter 25, verse 41. In this verse we find that when the final judgment day arrives, Satan and angels will be cast into the everlasting fire which God has prepared for them. Satan and his angels know this and this gives them a great incentive to destroy the lives of as many of mankind as they can before the final judgment day arrives.

The good angels submit to the will of God the Father and carry out His orders. When God expelled Adam and Eve from the garden of Eden we find in the book of Genesis, chapter 3, verse 24 that He sent cherubim and a flaming sword to guard the tree of life so they would not have access to it. When God decided to destroy Sodom and Gomorrah for their sinful ways we find in the book of Genesis, chapter 19, verses 1 through 24 He sent two of His angels to visit Lot to get him and his family out of the city before the destruction. When God decided His Son was to be born on earth we find in the book of Luke, chapter 1, verses 26 through 31 that He sent His angel Gabriel to tell Mary what was going to happen. When Jesus Christ was raised from the dead after His crucifixion we find in the book of Matthew, chapter 28, verse 2 God sent His angel to roll the stone away from the entrance.

## Prayer for the day:

Our Father in heaven above we understand that all the angels were originally created as good angels and by their own choice some of them became bad. We thank You for the good angels who do Your will and we thank You that You have control over the bad angels. We ask that You help us continue to do what You want us to do. We also ask that You limit our encounters with the bad angels. In the name of Jesus Christ we pray. Amen.

# Day #29
## Demons do not die.

Please open your Holy Bible to the book of Luke, chapter 20, verse 36 as we begin our study for the day.

When we consider demons as "fallen angels" we must also look at the attributes of the good angels. One of the attributes of the good angels is that they do not die. In the book of Luke, chapter 20, verse 36 you will find that those who believe in Jesus Christ and are part of His second coming will become like the good angels who do not die.

In the book of Matthew, chapter 25, verse 41 we find that Satan and his angels (demons) will be cast into the everlasting fire after they are judged by God for their evil deeds. Demons do not die and for the rest of eternity, after the final judgment, will be tormented in the everlasting fire. In the book of Revelation, chapter 20, verse 10 we find the deceiver Satan will be tormented every day, forever and ever after God passes His final judgment on him.

In the book of Hebrews, chapter 9, verse 27 we find that man is appointed to physically die once, after which he will be judged. Demons want you to be judged with sin in your life so you join them in the everlasting fire. Some scholars have said that man dies twice. The first death is the physical death and the second death is permanent separation from God if they do not have their faith and trust in Jesus Christ. Once a human being suffers physical death they don't get a second chance to choose between heaven and hell. You must choose while you are alive.

It is important for us to know angels and demons don't die. Both have been in existence from the day God created them to the very minute you are reading this. Angels have made a hobby of studying mankind. The biblical reference for the previous statement can be found in the Bible in the book of First Peter, chapter 1, verse 12. In this verse we clearly see that angels long to look into things. Demons also know many things about people that have existed and died through the many centuries and use this information to lure people into the occult through mediums. Demons don't know the future, but like angels have an extensive amount of knowledge about the past and how mankind reacts to certain situations.

Doctor Luke recorded in the book of Luke, chapter 16, verse 22 an incident where a beggar died and the good angles carried his soul to Abraham's side. This verse indicates to us that when a believer in Jesus Christ dies the good angels come and escort the person to where Abraham is, which is in heaven.

Prayer for the day:

Our Father in heaven above we thank You that if we believe in Your Son Jesus Christ we will become like the angels and will live for eternity with You. We ask that You help us walk in the way You want us to walk so we may some day worship You as the good angels do. In the name of Jesus Christ we pray. Amen.

# Day #30

At the end of today's reading you will be three quarters of the way to an understanding of demons.

## Demons do not marry.

Please open your Holy Bible to the book of Luke, chapter 20, verse 35 as we begin our study for the day.

When we say that demons do not marry we are again considering demons as "fallen angels". Looking at the attributes of the good angels we find that one of their attributes is that they do not marry. In the book of Luke, chapter 20, verse 35 you will find that those who believe in Jesus Christ and are part of His second coming will not marry or be given in marriage when they are in heaven. Continuing with Luke, chapter 20, verse 36 we see that believers in Jesus Christ will be like the angels. The fact that angels do not marry can also be found in the book of Matthew, chapter 22, verse 30 and also in the book of Mark, chapter 12, verse 25.

When wedding vows are exchanged and the words "till death do us part" are spoken we are emphasizing the fact that when one of a couple dies the one who remains is eligible to get married again. Their marriage does not continue in heaven even if both should eventually die having never remarried. We will be judged individually by God for whether or not we accepted or rejected His Son. The biblical reference for the previous statement can be found in the Bible in the book of John, chapter 12, verses 44 through 50. Whether or not we go to heaven or hell is our decision based on the fact that God has given us the freedom to choose whether or not to accept His Son. You may see your spouse in the same place you are sentenced to after God judges you, or you may not. Our hope and our prayer is that if you are married, both of you enjoy heaven for all eternity.

We have established the fact that angels do not marry based on verses we looked at in the Bible in the books of Matthew, Mark and Luke. We also established the fact that once we are in heaven we will be like the angels. In the book of Second Corinthians, chapter 6, verse 14 we find that we should not be unequally yoked together. If we look at this verse in the terms of marriage we could think of a Christian and a nonbeliever united in holy matrimony. The Christian in the marriage should be doing everything in his/her power to help the other person see the light. If you are currently in this situation our prayers are with you. Your Heavenly Father does not want to see anyone perish and neither do we.

Prayer for the day:

Our Father in heaven above we understand that Your angels do not marry and that we will be like Your angels after we leave this earth if we believe in Your Son. We ask that all who are married will together find a personal relationship with Your Son so they will both experience Your love in heaven. In the name of Jesus Christ we pray. Amen.

# Day #31
## Demons can be used by God for His purposes.

Please open your Holy Bible to the book of First Samuel, chapter 16, verse 14 as we begin our study for the day.

In the book of First Samuel, chapter 16, verse 14 we find that after the Spirit of the Lord left King Saul he was then tormented by an evil spirit. As we continue reading with verse 15 we find Saul's servants recognized the fact that an evil spirit was tormenting Saul. In verse 16 we find the demon visited Saul every now and then to torment him. In verse 23 we find when the evil spirit was tormenting Saul, if David played the harp, the evil spirit left Saul.

God in this instance used this particular demon to torment Saul. The demon in essence had God's permission to torment Saul. When we let sin into our lives and quench, or suppress, the Spirit of the Lord we are opening the door to be tormented. In the book of First Thessalonians, chapter 5, verse 19 we find that we are not to quench the Spirit. One of the ways we quench the Spirit is by saying "No" to God. Another way we quench the Spirit is when we fail to be submissive to God and attempt to do things our own way and not His way.

In the Bible in the book of Second Chronicles, chapter 18, verses 19 through 22 we find where a lying spirit was sent by the Lord to certain prophets to make those prophets liars. Since Satan is the father of all lies we can safely assume the lying spirit that was sent was probably one of Satan's demonic forces given permission by God to do His will.

In the book of Second Thessalonians, chapter 2, verse 11 we find God sending a strong delusion so the people believe lies. We know that Satan is the father of all lies and in this verse we see that God sent the delusion so the people would believe the lies. God is allowing Satan and his lying demons to have control over these people. He is using Satan and his demons to carry out His judgment.

One of the purposes of the good angels is to do God's will. One of the more common incidents where God used an angel to do His will can be found in the book of Matthew, chapter 28, verse 2. In this verse we find where God sent his angel to roll back the stone at the entrance of the tomb where Jesus Christ was placed after he was removed from the cross.

Another of the more common incidents can be found in the book of Luke, chapter 1, verses 26 through 38. In these verses we find God sent the angel Gabriel to Mary, the mother of Jesus, to tell her that she found favor in the eyes of God and that she was going to give birth to our Saviour.

God also uses His good angels to help those who have accepted the gift of salvation. In the book of Hebrews, chapter 1, verse 14 we find God uses His good angels as ministering spirits to those who have accepted his Son. Many people believe this verse indicates each believer in Jesus Christ has a guardian angel that watches over them.

Prayer for the day:
Our Father in heaven above we thank You that You are in control of both the bad angels and the good angels. We also thank You that in Your love for us You also show us mercy. We ask that You keep Your good angels close to us so they can help us make our journey through this life. In the name of Jesus Christ we pray. Amen.

# Day #32

## Demons can affect men, women, children, and animals.

Please open your Holy Bible to the book of Luke, chapter 4, verses 33 through 35 as we begin our study for the day.

In the book of Luke, chapter 4, verses 33 through 35 we find the story of a man who was affected by a demon. In this story we find a possessed man who was in the synagogue. When this man saw Jesus he yelled out that he knew that Jesus was the Holy One of God. Jesus told the demon residing in the man to be quiet and to leave the man. While the demon was departing from the man the demon threw the man to the ground. The man was not injured as the demon departed from him.

One of the best examples of a woman who at one point in her life was affected by not one but seven demons can be found in the book of Luke, chapter 8, verse 2. This verse clearly tells us Mary Magdalene at one point in her life was possessed by seven demons. Jesus chased the demons from her and she chose to follow Jesus as He ministered to the people.

An example of a child who was demon possessed can be found in the book of Luke, chapter 9, verses 38 through 42. In these verses we find a father who is concerned for the health of his son asking Jesus for His help. This young boy would cry out and foam at the mouth while the demon possessed him. The demon would also bruise the child. The disciples could not cast out the demon from the boy because of their lack of faith. Jesus chastised the disciples for their lack of faith and cast the demon out of the boy. Jesus gave the child back to his father after the demon was removed.

Another example of a child who was demon possessed can be found in the Bible in the book of Mark, chapter 7, verses 25 through 30. In these verses we find a mother who was concerned for the health of her daughter. In verse 25 she falls at the feet of Jesus and in verse 26 she keeps asking Him to remove the demon from her daughter. In verse 29 Jesus tells her the demon is gone from her daughter and in verse 30 we find that when the mother returned home the demon was indeed gone.

Demons can enter and possess animals. An example of demons possessing animals can be found in the book of Matthew, chapter 8, verse 31. In this verse we see the demons begging Jesus to send them into the herd of swine after they were chased from the demon possessed man. This incident was also recorded in the book of Mark, chapter 5, verse 12, and in the book of Luke, chapter 8, verse 32.

Angels can interact with men, women, children, and even animals.

It has been recorded in the Bible in the book of Matthew, chapter 1, verse 20 where and angel spoke to Joseph, the earthly father of Jesus Christ, in a dream.

Recorded in the book of Luke, chapter 1, verses 26 through 38 is the story of an angel of God speaking to Mary, the mother of Jesus Christ, and telling her about the son she was going to give birth to.

In the book of Matthew, chapter 18, verse 10 we are led to believe that children have their own personal guardian angel.

In the book of Daniel, chapter 6, verse 22 we find an angel was sent by God to keep the mouths of the lions closed so they could not harm Daniel after he was cast into the den of lions.

Prayer for the day:
Our Father in heaven above we acknowledge the fact demons can affect men, women, children, and animals. We also acknowledge that

Your angels can interact with all of Your creation to do Your will. We ask that You help us walk in Your light always and thank You again for Your good angels. In the name of Jesus Christ we pray. Amen.

# Day #33

## Demons have easy access to a person when sin is present in their life.

Please open your Holy Bible to the book of John, chapter 5, verses 5 through 14 as we begin our study for the day.

In the book of John, chapter 5, verses 5 through 14 we find the story of a man who had been sick for thirty eight years. In verse 8 we find Jesus took compassion on the man and healed him. In verse 14 Jesus tells the man not to sin any more because if he does he could get sicker than he originally was. From this story we see that once sin enters a life the person is easily susceptible to demonic influences.

Looking at a definition of sin we could say that sin in breaking the rules that God has established. A biblical reference for the previous statement can be found in the book of First John, chapter 3, verse 4. Also in First John, chapter 5, verse 19 we find that Satan is currently influencing the people in the world to sin against God. It is recorded in the book of Job, chapter 34, verses 21 and 22 God sees every step a sinner takes and nothing a sinner does is hidden from God.

Stop and consider that the Bible tells us in the book of Romans, chapter 3, verse 23 we all have sinned and fall short of the glory of God. When we consider this verse it is easy to realize we can be demonically influenced every minute of our life until we accept Jesus

Christ as our personal Saviour. Also in the book of Romans, chapter 5, verse 8 we find that while we were yet sinners Jesus Christ died for our sins. Continuing in the book of Romans, chapter 6, verse 23 we are told that the wages for our sins is death. This death is separation from God and His love forever. Verse 23 also tells us that we can have the gift of eternal life with God by accepting His Son, Jesus Christ, as our Lord.

When we consider angels with reference to this topic we are comforted by the fact that in the Bible in the book of Hebrews, chapter 1, verse 14 God sends His angels to help all those who have accepted His Son. Lack of sin in our lives is pleasing to our Heavenly Father and once we accept His Son the Holy Spirit moves into our life and the angels are there to help and protect us. In the book of First John, chapter 1, verse 9 we find if we confess our sins God is faithful to forgive us. It is comforting to know that Jesus promised us in the book of Hebrews, chapter 13, verse 5 He would never leave us or forsake us. In the book of Philippians, chapter 4, verse 13 we find we can accomplish all things with the strength that Jesus Christ gives.

Prayer for the day:
Our Father in heaven above we thank You that You sent Your Son to die on the cross for our sins and once we accept Your Son, the Holy Spirit moves into our life. We know that Satan will attack us even more once we accept Your Son but we also know You are more powerful than him. We ask that You help us with our daily walk through life, that we live the way You want us to. In the name of Jesus Christ we pray. Amen.

# Day #34
## Demons have the ability to travel.

Please open your Holy Bible to the book of Matthew, chapter 12, verse 44 as we begin our study for the day.

In the book of Matthew, chapter 12, verse 44 we find once a demon leaves a person the demon travels around, seeking to find rest. If the demon doesn't find a new place to rest, he will go back to the place that he originally left.

Doctor Luke writes in the book of Luke, chapter 24, verse 39 that Jesus said a spirit does not have flesh and bones. We can see flesh and bones, but we can not see a spirit. In Luke, chapter 4, verse 35 we find a demon traveling from a man that he possessed, sight unseen. Also in Luke, chapter 8 verse 33 we find a "Legion" of demons traveling from a man to enter a herd of pigs, sight unseen.

We know from the book of First Peter, chapter 5, verse 8 Satan travels around like a roaring lion seeking whom he may destroy. If sin in your life has opened the door for him he will enter in with the goal to destroy you.

According to the Bible in the book of Genesis, chapter 1, verses 26 and 27 you are made in the image of God. Since you are made in the image of God, Satan wants to destroy you because you remind him of God every time he looks at you. Satan really enjoys destroying an image of God.

Angels have the ability to travel back and forth between heaven and earth. They function as messengers between God in heaven and mankind on earth. In the book of Matthew, chapter 4, verse 11 we find angels ministering to Jesus Christ after Satan tempted Him three times in the wilderness. Also in the book of Matthew, chapter 28, verse 2 we find where an angel traveled from heaven to the tomb where the body of Jesus was laid to roll back the stone.

In the book of Genesis, chapter 16, verse 7 we find an angel traveled from heaven to find Hagar and tell her to go back and submit to Sarai (Sarah). Also in the book of Genesis, chapter 19, verse 1 we find two angels traveled from heaven to the gate at Sodom to meet Lot.

In the book of Judges, chapter 13, verse 3, we find an angel traveled from heaven to earth to talk with Samson's mother. It should be noted that angels stay around long enough to deliver their message from God and then depart. Demons on the other hand travel all around earth seeking to separate mankind from God their Creator.

Prayer for the day:

Our Father in heaven above we thank You that You gave Your creations the ability to travel and enjoy all You have created. We know that demons travel around seeking whom they can destroy and we ask that once we accept Your Son that You give us the strength and ability to continue to serve You. In the name of Jesus Christ we pray. Amen.

# Day #35

## Demons know that Jesus Christ is the Son of God.

Please open your Holy Bible to the book of Mark, chapter 1, verses 23 and 24 as we begin our study for the day.

There are several instances recorded in the Bible where demons shout out that Jesus Christ is the Son of God. In the book of Mark, chapter 1, verses 23 and 24 we find a man in the synagogue that was demonically influenced. This demon cried out to Jesus to let him alone because he knew Jesus could destroy him. The demon knew that Jesus was the Holy One of God. This incident was also recorded by Doctor Luke in the book of Luke, chapter 4, verses 33 through 35. Continuing in the book of Mark with chapter 1 and verse 34 we find Jesus would not allow the demons to speak because they knew who He was. Also in the book of Mark, chapter 5, verse 7 we find a demon possessed man calling out to Jesus and calling Him the Son of God. This demon asked Jesus not to torment him. Quite an event when we find a demon that was doing the tormenting asking not to be tormented by the Son of God.

In the book of Luke, chapter 4, verse 41 we find many demons were cast out of people. Jesus would not allow the demons to speak because they knew Jesus Christ was the Son of God. If we back up one verse to verse 40 it is interesting to note that all of the people who were sick with many different types of illnesses were healed by Jesus with the touch of His hands.

Once we know that the bad angels know Jesus is the Son of God we can safely assume that the good angels know also. In the Bible in the book of Matthew, chapter 16, verse 27 we find that when Jesus comes back to earth again He will be coming with His angels. Also in Matthew, chapter 25, verse 31 we find that Jesus is coming back with all of the good angels.

In the book of Psalms, chapter 148, verse 2 we find that all the angels in heaven praise the Lord. In the book of Hebrews, chapter 1, verse 6 we find that when God sends His Son back to earth all of God's angels will worship the Son.

### Prayer for the day:

Our Father in heaven above we thank You for Your Son. We thank You that He died on the cross for our sins. We acknowledge that both the bad and good angels know Your Son and respect His power. We ask that You help us be ready for Your Son's second coming when He comes back to earth with all of His angels. In the name of Jesus Christ we pray. Amen.

# Day #36
## Demons possess different degrees of wickedness.

Please open your Holy Bible to the book of Matthew, chapter 12, verse 45 as we begin our study for the day.

In the book of Matthew, chapter 12, verse 45 we find where demonic degrees of wickedness are mentioned. The verse indicates that the demon returning back to the person he left returned with seven demons that were more wicked than him. This could be a good explanation for the noticeable difference in people that some are more wicked than others.

In the book of Mark, chapter 9, verse 29 we find some demons are so powerful they can only be removed by a combination of prayer and fasting.

The more demons that are influencing a person the more wicked they will appear to be.

Even though demons have varying degrees of wickedness they share common goals. They want to keep you from a personal relationship with Jesus Christ and will do everything in their power to keep from finding Him. They also want you to spend the rest of eternity with them in hell after the great judgment.

There are several different types of angels found in the Bible such as cherubim, seraphim, and archangels. Cherubim can be found in the book of Genesis, chapter 3, verse 24. They are considered to be guardians as found in the account of Adam and Eve and the tree of life. Seraphim can be found in the book of Isaiah, chapter 6, verses 2 and 6 and are viewed as serving God as worshipers and obedient servants. Archangels can be found in the book of Jude, chapter 1, verse 9 and in First Thessalonians, chapter 4, verse 16 and are viewed as having more power than an angel.

The word angel is associated with the word messenger and they indeed are God's messengers as indicated in the book of Acts, chapter 10, verses 3 through 7. In these verses we find an angel was sent from God in a vision to Cornelius to give him instructions for what he must do.

Angels can be fighters as evidenced in the book of Jude, chapter 1, verse 9 when the archangel Michael disputed with Satan about the body of Moses. What is interesting in this verse is that the archangel Michael did not rebuke Satan but stated the Lord should rebuke him.

Angels can be guardians as evidenced in the Psalms, chapter 91, verses 11 and 12. In these two verses we see that God will send his angels to guard you so you don't get hurt.

Prayer for the day:

Our Father in heaven above we understand that some demons are more wicked than others. We also understand that angels have different responsibilities, some are messengers and some are fighters. We ask that You help us to stay away from sin so we can avoid some of the demonic attacks. In the name of Jesus Christ we pray. Amen.

# Day #37

## Demons can masquerade as good spirits.

Please open your Holy Bible to the book of Second Corinthians, chapter 11, verse 15 as we begin our study for the day.

In the book of Second Corinthians, chapter 11, verse 15 we find that Satan's ministers transform themselves into ministers of righteousness. From this verse we can conclude that demons are able to masquerade as good spirits.

This topic becomes important when you relate it to psychics. A psychic is believed by some to contact the spirits of the dead. Who is to say that the "conjured up" spirits are not demons, the bad spirits? Demons have been in existence since the day God created them and they may know your friends and relatives both dead and alive. Demons can answer specific questions about a dead person because they existed along with that person when the dead person was alive. We are told in the book of Isaiah, chapter 8, verses 19 and 20 it is foolish and sinful to conjure up spirits when we have a living God whom we can consult.

In the book of First Samuel, chapter 28, verses 7 through 19 we find the story of the "Witch of Endor" who conjured up a spirit. When we look at verse 12 we find the witch was surprised when she did. This witch did not encounter a demon posing as the prophet Samuel. The answer to her request, in this incident, was God giving permission to Samuel to visit the witch and King Saul. This is the first of two incidents in the Bible where God gave a deceased person permission to visit mankind. The other incident can be found in the book of Matthew, chapter 17, verse 3 where we find Moses and Elijah standing with Jesus Christ, the Son of God.

Angels do not have to masquerade as good spirits because they are good spirits. The purpose of a masquerade is to deceive. The good angels do not deceive mankind because they are God's messengers and God does not deceive. If you were given the opportunity to see an angel could you tell whether or not it was truly a good angel or a demon masquerading as a good angel? We know from the Bible in the book of Second Corinthians, chapter 11, verse 15 that demons can masquerade as good spirits. The safest approach you can take is not to go looking for angels. You will save yourself all of the problems associated with a demon posing as a good angel.

Prayer for the day:
Our Father in heaven above we thank You that Your good angels do not have to masquerade as anything to do Your will. We ask Your help to stay away from the psychics of this world and rely on prayer to You for all our needs and wants. In the name of Jesus Christ we pray. Amen.

# Day #38
## Demons can trouble a person and not possess (enter) the person.

Please open your Holy Bible to the book of First Samuel, chapter 16, verses 14 through 23 as we begin our study for the day.

In the book of First Samuel, chapter 16, verses 14 through 23 we find a spirit tormenting King Saul. It is interesting to note that God allowed the spirit to torment Saul. In verse 14 we find that once the Spirit of God departed from Saul the tormenting spirit took up temporary residency. This story adds credence to the fact that evil spirits can only do what God allows them to do.

In verse 23 we find that when the evil spirit was harassing King Saul, if David played the harp the evil spirit departed from King Saul. There is no doubt God told the evil spirit to depart from King Saul when David played the harp. The music alone did not remove the spirit but the hand of God removed the spirit. God is in full control of every situation, both the good ones and the bad ones.

We are not going to tell you that demons are behind every physical problem or abnormality. The possibility does exist that demonic influence could be behind some physical problems, as long as they have God's permission to do so. Physical problems that can not be traced to physical causes would be suspect to demonic influences at work.

Angels do not trouble a person unless they are directed by God to do so. They do not possess (enter) a person because they are capable of presenting themselves in human form. One example of an angel appearing in human form in the Bible can be found in the book of Mark, chapter 16, verse 5. This angel appears as a young man dressed in a long white robe. In the book of Matthew, chapter 28, verse 3 we find this angel at the tomb of the resurrected Jesus Christ. His countenance was like lighting and his clothing was as white as snow. Continuing with verse 4 we find that when the guards at the tomb took one look at the angel they fainted in fear.

If you are a Christian and God has allowed you to be troubled He does not stop thinking about you during that time. God has given you a promise that is recorded in the book of First Corinthians, chapter 10, verse 13 that He won't allow you to be troubled more than you can bear. We find great comfort in that promise. Recorded in the book of Mark, chapter 10, verse 27 is another promise that all things are possible if we would just believe in the power of God our Heavenly Father.

Prayer for the day:
Our Father in heaven above we thank You that when the Holy Spirit is living inside of us we are at peace with ourselves. We understand Satan and his demons can still attack us but we remain comforted by the fact that You are more powerful than they are. We ask that You help us keep our eyes on You and to resist the tricks and deceitfulness of Satan and his demons. In the name of Jesus Christ we pray. Amen.

# Day #39
## Demons can leave a body and then return again.

Please open your Holy Bible to the book of Matthew, chapter 12, verses 43 through 45 as we begin our study for the day.

In the book of Matthew, chapter 12, verses 43 through 45 we find a demon, "unclean spirit", can leave a person and then return again. According to these verses the demon leaves the person, looks for a place to rest, finds none, and then returns again. When the demon returns again to the person he may take seven more demons with him. The seven additional demons that he returns with are more wicked than him. Also in the Bible, Doctor Luke in the book of Luke, chapter 11, verses 24 through 26 records the same information.

It is important for us to realize that sin in our lives opens the door to demonic influences. The sin, repeated over and over again, keeps the door open for more demons to join in. When we accept Jesus Christ as our personal Saviour we close the door on the demons and open to door to the Holy Spirit. If we grieve the Holy Spirit, and His ministry is "quenched" in us, we instantly open the door again not to a demon but several demons.

A reference to blasphemy against the Holy Spirit can be found in the Bible in the book of Matthew, chapter 12, verses 31 and 32. These verses indicate to us there is an unforgivable sin we do not want to commit which is blasphemy against the Holy Spirit. An additional reference found in the book of Mark, chapter 3, verse 29 states blasphemy will never will be forgiven and is subject to eternal condemnation. The sin of blasphemy against the Holy Spirit will open the door to demonic influences on a fill time basis and will result in eternal condemnation.

Angels acting as messengers for God have returned to the same person on several occasions. In the Bible in the book of Matthew, chapter 1, verse 20 we find an angel informing Joseph he should take Mary as his wife. In the book of Matthew, chapter 2, verse 13 we find an angel telling Joseph to take his family and go to Egypt. In Matthew, chapter 2, verse 20 we find an angel telling Joseph to take his family and go back to Israel. Angels are messengers from God and will go back to the same person as many times as God tells them to.

In the Old Testament of the Bible, in the book of Judges, chapter 13, verse 3 we find an angel talking to the mother of Samson. The angel explained to the wife of Manoah that she was going to give birth to a son. Continuing with verse 4 we see the angel also told her not to drink any wine or strong drink and not to eat anything that was unclean. In verses 6 and 7 she explains the event to Manoah. As we continue with verses 8 through 20 we see that Manoah prayed that the angel return. The angel did return. Manoah conversed with the angel, offered an offering to the Lord, and the angel ascended in the flame. What is interesting in these verses is verse 16 where this angel would not eat and verse 18 where this angel would not tell his name because it was a secret.

Prayer for the day:
Our Father in heaven above we learned from these verses that demons can leave a person and then return. We ask Your help to keep our house clean so we don't have any unclean spirits trying to take residency. In the name of Jesus Christ we pray. Amen.

# Day #40

At the end of today's reading we hope that you have an understanding of demons.

## Demons can't make you do anything you don't want to do.

Please open your Holy Bible to the book of Philippians, chapter 4, verse 13 as we begin our study for the day.

It is important for us to realize as we finish this study that demons can't make us do anything we don't want to do. God has given us the ability to choose. We can choose either to worship God or worship Satan.

The list of powers Satan has does not include the ability to force you to do anything. He certainly can make the sinful things look real appealing, but you must choose.

In the book of Philippians, chapter 4, verse 13 we find you can do all things with the help of Jesus Christ who will give you the strength you will need. In the book of First John, chapter 4, verse 4 we find that once you accept Jesus Christ as your personal Saviour, greater is Jesus that lives inside you than Satan who lives in the world.

Angels do what God tells them to do. The reference for the previous statement can be found in the Bible in the book of Psalms, chapter 103, verse 20. This verse tells us the angles listen to God and He tells them what to do and they do it. The good angels can not make you do anything either. You have the freedom to choose between good and evil. The choices you make come complete with consequences. If you choose to believe that Jesus Christ is God's Son and are sorry for your sins you will be on the path to everlasting life. If you choose to follow the things of this world and Satan you will be on the path to the everlasting fire.

In the book of Isaiah, chapter 55, verse 6 we are told to seek our Saviour while He may be found and to call upon Him. Take heed to these words and seek a relationship with Jesus Christ before He comes again to this earth or it will truly be too late. God gave His angels a choice and He is giving you a choice, heaven or the everlasting fire. The demons are going to the everlasting fire and want you to join them. Jesus wants you to follow Him and go to heaven. Choose wisely.

Prayer for the day:

Our Father in heaven above, on this the last day of our study, we thank You that You gave us freedom of choice. We ask that You help us choose wisely in everything we do and say. In the name of Jesus Christ we pray. Amen.

# Day #41

I know we said 40 days but let's discuss one more topic.

## Do you think that you are being demonically influenced?

Please open your Holy Bible to the book of Isaiah, chapter 55, verse 6 as we begin.

If you are not a believer in Jesus Christ then call upon Him while He may be found. (Isaiah, chapter 55, verse 6) Jesus will come to you if you call upon Him in an honest and truthful way. (Psalm, chapter 145, verse 18)

Call upon the name of Jesus and ask for forgiveness of your sins. (First John, chapter 1, verse 9) Whoever calls upon Jesus Christ and confesses He is the Lord, and that He was raised from the dead, will be saved. (Romans, chapter 10, verses 9 and 13)

If you are a Christian and feel you are being attacked by Satan and his followers what can you do?

Examine your life to see that the things you are doing, and the way you are living, are pleasing your Heavenly Father. Do you trust in Jesus with all your heart for everything that you do? Do you trust on your own intuition instead of trusting Him? If you trust Jesus for all that you do He will help you with your decisions. (Proverbs, chapter 3, verses 5 and 6) Sin in your life is a serious problem and sin repeated is an open invitation for demonic attacks. Confess the sin, or sins, and get right with God.

Remember God's promise He won't put any trial or tribulation in front of you that you and He can't handle together. (First Corinthians, chapter 10, verse 13) Just because you are a Christian doesn't mean there won't be any trials and tribulations in your life. Rest assured that God is always there for you. Your God will never leave you or forsake you. (Hebrews, chapter 13, verse 5)

Prayer for the day:

Our Father in heaven above we thank You that You sent Your Son to die on the cross for our sins. We know that You are more powerful than all of Your creation and that You will never leave us or forsake us. Please help us pray frequently, and trust in you for all of our needs. In the name of Jesus Christ we pray. Amen.

# Conclusion

We hope, and pray, you enjoyed our study together as we looked at demons, the good angels, and prayed a simple prayer for forty days. It is believed by some that forty consecutive days of focusing on a topic is enough time to cause a change in a person's life.

Throughout this study we tried to show you a loving God, His forgiving Son, a lying and deceitful Satan, and Satan's demonic followers.

Always remember once you accept Jesus Christ as your personal Saviour that greater is He that lives in you than Satan who lives in the world. (First John, chapter 4, verse 4) As we previously stated, and it's worth stating again, no matter how bad things seem to get in your life remember God will not put any problems in your life that you and He can not handle together. (First Corinthians, chapter 10, verse 13)

We hope, and pray, you learned through this study that God is real, Jesus Christ is real, the Holy Spirit is real, angels are real, Satan is real, demons are real, and every person created exists today and for all eternity. All those that worship and serve Jesus will be going to heaven, and all those that worship and serve Satan will be going to hell. The choice is yours. As we stated before, choose wisely. If you submit yourself to God your Father and resist the devil he will run away from you. (James, chapter 4, verse 7)

May God bless you as you journey through this life trusting in Him. Amen.